THE ESSENTIAL WISDOM OF THE WORLD'S GREATEST LEADERS

THE
ESSENTIAL
WISDOM
OF THE
WORLD'S
GREATEST
LEADERS

EDITED BY
CAROL KELLY-GANGI

FALL RIVER PRESS

New York

To my son, John Christopher, with much love

FALL RIVER PRESS

New York

An Imprint of Sterling Publishing Co., Inc.
1166 Avenue of the Americas
New York, NY 10036

ISBN 978-1-4351-6824-4

Distributed in Canada by Sterling Publishing Co., Inc.
c/o Canadian Manda Group, 664 Annette Street
Toronto, Ontario M6S 2C8, Canada
Distributed in the United Kingdom by GMC Distribution Services
Castle Place, 166 High Street, Lewes, East Sussex BN7 1XU, England
Distributed in Australia by NewSouth Books
45 Beach Street, Coogee, NSW 2034, Australia

For information about custom editions, special sales, and premium and
corporate purchases, please contact Sterling Special Sales at 800-805-5489
or specialsales@sterlingpublishing.com.

Manufactured in the United States of America

2 4 6 8 10 9 7 5 3

sterlingpublishing.com

CONTENTS

✳   ✳   ✳   ✳   ✳

INTRODUCTION

✳   ✳   ✳   ✳   ✳

What makes someone a great leader? Researchers point to traits such as intelligence, self-confidence, determination, integrity, sociability, and emotional intelligence as qualities that have an impact on one's ability to be a successful leader. There is certainly deep division in our own country and around the world about who on the world stage is worthy of being deemed a great leader—or even a good leader. Indeed, history suggests that it can take decades to achieve clarity and consensus on who will be remembered as a truly great leader. In the meantime, why not take some time away from the pundits and peddlers and revisit the words of hundreds of remarkable leaders who have each profoundly shaped our world from antiquity to the present day.

Who are these great leaders? Within these pages you will find presidents and prime ministers; saints and scientists; politicians and philosophers; judges and generals; activists and athletes; investors and inventors; professors and poets; and statesmen and scholars. It is hoped that the words of these extraordinary men and women will cut across the boundaries of time and place to form an open discourse on leadership.

In the selections that follow, Mahatma Gandhi, Martin Luther King, Jr., Nelson Mandela, Golda Meir, Sandra Day O'Connor, and Lao Tzu each reflect on the meaning of leadership. Elsewhere, Hillary Rodham Clinton, Benjamin Disraeli, Frederick Douglass, and Colin Powell exchange ideas about the supremacy of law, the quest for equality, and the demands of justice. Alexander the Great, Julius Caesar, Winston Churchill, Queen Elizabeth I, and Franklin D. Roosevelt each deliver rousing exhortations to victory during the dark days of war. Meanwhile, the Dalai Lama, Indira Gandhi, Pope Francis, Barack

Obama, and Eleanor Roosevelt reflect on the sobering realities of achieving peace.

Throughout this inspiring book, these leaders and others reflect on universal themes such as the undying love of family; the meaning of hardship, adversity, and hope; the path to achievement; and the role of religion, morality, and virtue in our lives and in the world.

It is my hope that experiencing the words of some of the world's greatest leaders will help to inspire, challenge, and empower us as we travel our own path to wisdom.

—CAROL KELLY-GANGI
2018

WHAT IS LEADERSHIP?

Leadership and learning are indispensable to each other.

—**John F. Kennedy**

Sheryl Sandberg

The ability to learn is the most important quality a leader can have.

—**Sheryl Sandberg**

A genuine leader is not a searcher for consensus but a molder of consensus.

—**Martin Luther King, Jr.**

A true leader has the confidence to stand alone, the courage to make tough decisions, and the compassion to listen to the needs of others. He does not set out to be a leader but becomes one by the equality of his actions and the integrity of his intent.

—**Douglas MacArthur**

The real leader displays his quality in his triumphs over adversity, however great it may by.

—**George C. Marshall**

There comes a time when one must take a position that is neither safe, nor politic, nor popular, but he must take it because conscience tells him it is right.

—Martin Luther King, Jr.

Leadership to me means duty, honor, country. It means character, and it means listening from time to time.

—George W. Bush

All of the great leaders have had one characteristic in common: it was the willingness to confront unequivocally the major anxiety of their people in their time.

—John Kenneth Galbraith

Great leaders are almost always great simplifiers, who can cut through argument, debate, and doubt to offer a solution everybody can understand.

—Colin Powell

Leadership is fired in the forge of ambition and opportunity.

—James MacGregor Burns

I suppose leadership at one time meant muscles; but today it means getting along with people.

—Mahatma Gandhi

You do not lead by hitting people over the head—that's assault, not leadership.

—**Dwight D. Eisenhower**

I love to see honest and honorable men at the helm, men who will not bend their politics to their purses nor pursue measures by which they may profit and then profit by their measures.

—**Thomas Jefferson**

I am an organizer, not a union leader. A good organizer has to work hard and long. There are no shortcuts. You just keep talking to people, working with them, sharing, exchanging and they come along.

—**Cesar Chavez**

I am not interested in power for power's sake, but I'm interested in power that is moral, that is right, and that is good.

—**Martin Luther King, Jr.**

The task of the leader is always to weigh up the circumstances, to make decisions and to give orders and then, once the action has been launched, to reassess from time to time the system of the means at his disposal, which [is] continually being modified by circumstances.

—**Charles de Gaulle**

He who exercises government by means of his virtue may be compared to the north polar star, which keeps its place and all the stars turn towards it.

—**Confucius**

Men make history and not the other way around. In periods where there is no leadership, society stands still. Progress occurs when courageous, skillful leaders seize the opportunity to change things for the better.

—**Harry S. Truman**

Divide and rule, the politician cries;
Unite and lead, is watchword of the wise.

—**Johann Wolfgang von Goethe**

My own definition of leadership is this: The capacity and the will to rally men and women in a common purpose, and the character which inspires confidence.

—**Bernard Montgomery**

A leader is a dealer in hope.

—**Napoleon Bonaparte**

Leaders should be collaborative, modest, and generous.

—**Bill Bradley**

Leadership is the art of getting someone else to do something you want done because he wants to do it.

—**Dwight D. Eisenhower**

Sandra Day O'Connor.

In order to cultivate a set of leaders with legitimacy in the eyes of the citizenry, it is necessary that the path to leadership be visibly open to talented and qualified individuals of every race and ethnicity.

—**Sandra Day O'Connor**

Leadership has a harder job to do than just choose sides. It must bring sides together.

—**Jesse Jackson**

To lead people, walk behind them.

—**Lao Tzu**

I must follow the people. Am I not their leader?

—**Benjamin Disraeli**

In Iroquois society, leaders are encouraged to remember seven generations in the past and consider seven generations in the future when making decisions that affect the people.

—**Wilma Mankiller**

It is better to lead from behind and to put others in front, especially when you celebrate victory when nice things occur. You take the front line when there is danger. Then people will appreciate your leadership.

—**Nelson Mandela**

Woe to him that claims obedience when it is not due; woe to him that refuses it when it is.

—**Thomas Carlyle**

If you just set out to be liked, you would be prepared to compromise on anything at any time, and you would achieve nothing.

—**Margaret Thatcher**

Leadership does not always wear the harness of compromise.

—**Woodrow Wilson**

No man will make a great leader who wants to do it all himself, or to get all the credit for doing it.

—**Andrew Carnegie**

A good leader is a person who takes a little more than his share of the blame and a little less than his share of the credit.

—**John C. Maxwell**

All leadership takes place through the communication of ideas to the minds of others.

—**Charles Cooley**

I start with the premise that the function of leadership is to produce more leaders, not followers.

—**Ralph Nader**

A competent leader can get efficient service from poor troops, while on the contrary an incapable leader can demoralize the best of troops.

—**John J. Pershing**

A leader who doesn't hesitate before he sends his nation into battle is not fit to be a leader.

—**Golda Meir**

No nation can safely trust its martial honor to leaders who do not maintain the universal code which distinguishes between those things that are right and those things that are wrong.

—**Douglas MacArthur**

In the future, there will be no female leaders. There will just be leaders.

—**Sheryl Sandberg**

A true leader always keeps an element of surprise up his sleeve, which others cannot grasp but which keeps his public excited and breathless.

—**Charles de Gaulle**

In government institutions and in teaching, you need to inspire confidence. To achieve credibility, you have to very clearly explain what you are doing and why.

—**Janet Yellen**

Leadership should be born out of the understanding of the needs of those who would be affected by it.

—**Marian Anderson**

True leadership stems from individuality that is honestly and sometimes imperfectly expressed. . . . Leaders should strive for authenticity over perfection.

—**Sheryl Sandberg**

Leadership is solving problems. The day soldiers stop bringing you their problems is the day you have stopped leading them. They have either lost confidence that you can help or concluded you do not care. Either case is a failure of leadership.

—**Colin Powell**

As a leader, I am tough on myself and I raise the standard for everybody; however, I am very caring because I want people to excel at what they are doing so that they can aspire to be me in the future.

—Indra Nooyi

Leadership is the capacity to translate vision into reality.

—Warren Bennis

One of the key elements of being a good business leader is the capacity to tell the hard truths.

—Jeff Bezos

Leadership is a potent combination of strategy and character. But if you must be without one, be without the strategy.

—H. Norman Schwarzkopf, Jr.

Leadership cannot just go along to get along. . . . Leadership must meet the moral challenge of the day.

—Jesse Jackson

KNOWLEDGE, EDUCATION, AND INNOVATION

Knowledge will forever govern ignorance; and a people who mean to be their own governors must arm themselves with the power which knowledge gives.

—James Madison

The pursuit of knowledge itself implies a world where men are free to follow out the logic of their own ideas. It implies a world where nations are free to solve their own problems and to realize their own ideals.

—John F. Kennedy

You can imprison a man, but not an idea. You can exile a man, but not an idea. You can kill a man, but not an idea.

—Benazir Bhutto

Knowledge—like the sky—is never private property. No teacher has a right to withhold it from anyone who asks for it. Teaching is the art of sharing.

—Abraham Joshua Heschel

No man and no force can take from the world the books that embody man's eternal fight against tyranny of every kind. In this war, we know, books are weapons. And it is a part of your dedication always to make them weapons for man's freedom.

—**Franklin D. Roosevelt**

Once you learn to read, you will be forever free.

—**Frederick Douglass**

The Master said, Yu, shall I teach you what knowledge is? When you know a thing, to recognize that you know it, and when you do not know a thing, to recognize that you do not know it. That is knowledge.

—**Confucius**

To be conscious that you are ignorant is a great step to knowledge.

—**Benjamin Disraeli**

A Bible and a newspaper in every house, a good school in every district—all studied and appreciated as they merit—are the principal support of virtue, morality, and civil liberty.

—**Benjamin Franklin**

What is the good of experience if you do not reflect?

—**Frederick the Great**

Knowledge—that is, education in its true sense—is our best protection against unreasoning prejudice and panic-making fear, whether engendered by special interests, illiberal minorities, or panic-stricken leaders.

—**Franklin D. Roosevelt**

Knowledge begets knowledge. The more I see, the more impressed I am—not with how much we know, but with how tremendous the areas are that are as yet unexplored.

—**John Glenn**

I was brought up to believe that the only thing worth doing was to add to the sum of accurate information in the world.

—**Margaret Mead**

Anyone who stops learning is old, whether at twenty or eighty. Anyone who keeps learning stays young. The greatest thing in life is to keep your mind young.

—**Henry Ford**

In some places of the world, students are going to school every day. It's their normal life. But in other parts of the world, we are starving for education . . . it's like a precious gift. It's like a diamond.

—**Malala Yousafzai**

Without education, you are not going anywhere in this world.

—Malcolm X

Next in importance to freedom and justice is popular education, without which neither freedom nor justice can be permanently maintained.

—James A. Garfield

Mankind have been created for the sake of one another. Either instruct them, therefore, or endure them.

—Marcus Aurelius

A teacher who is attempting to teach without inspiring the pupil with a desire to learn is hammering on cold iron.

—Horace Mann

One looks back with appreciation to the brilliant teachers, but with gratitude to those who touched our human feelings. The curriculum is so much necessary raw material, but warmth is the vital element for the growing plant and for the soul of the child.

—Carl Jung

Education's purpose is to replace an empty mind with an open one.

—Malcolm S. Forbes

Education, more than any single force, will mold the citizen of the future. The classroom—not the trench—is the frontier of freedom.

—**Lyndon B. Johnson**

Sparking someone's love of learning, changing the course of a life, standing up for the freedom to read, to learn. Nothing is more important than that in a free society.

—**Hillary Rodham Clinton**

It is time for every child to understand that if they study hard and take their school work seriously, they will be able to get a higher education, regardless of their family's income. It's time to reduce the outrageous burden of student debt that is weighing down the lives of millions of college graduates.

—**Bernie Sanders**

Let us remember: One book, one pen, one child, and one teacher can change the world.

—**Malala Yousafzai**

I think that education is power. I think that being able to communicate with people is power. One of my main goals on the planet is to encourage people to empower themselves.

—**Oprah Winfrey**

The sage does not hoard. Having bestowed all he has on others, he has yet more; having given all he has to others, he is richer still.

—**Lao Tzu**

Education is not preparation for life; education is life itself.

—**John Dewey**

Education is the most powerful weapon which you can use to change the world.

—**Nelson Mandela**

Never tell people how to do things. Tell them what to do and they will surprise you with their ingenuity.

—**George S. Patton**

The open society, the unrestricted access to knowledge, the unplanned and uninhibited association of men for its furtherance—these are what may make a vast, complex, ever-growing, ever-changing, ever more specialized and expert technological world, nevertheless a world of human community.

—**J. Robert Oppenheimer**

We are all now connected by the Internet, like neurons in a giant brain.

—**Stephen Hawking**

You guys are the magicians of the twenty-first century. Don't let anything hold you back. Imagination is the limit. Go out there and create some magic.

—**Elon Musk**

TRUTH

The first duty of a man is the seeking after, and the investigation of truth.

—Cicero

A man who seeks truth and loves it must be reckoned precious to any human society.

—Frederick the Great

To love truth is the principal part of human perfection in this world, and the seed-plot of all other virtues.

—John Locke

Facts are stubborn things; and whatever may be our wishes, our inclinations, or the dictates of our passions, they cannot alter the state of facts and evidence.

—John Adams

Every truth we see is one to give to the world, not to keep to ourselves alone.

—Elizabeth Cady Stanton

He who permits himself to tell a lie once, finds it much easier to do it a second and third time, till at length it becomes habitual; he tells lies without attending to it, and truths without the world's believing him. This falsehood of the tongue leads to that of the heart, and in time depraves all its good dispositions.

—Thomas Jefferson

False words are not only evil in themselves, but they infect the soul with evil.

—Socrates

Ethical truth is as exact and as peremptory as physical truth.

—Herbert Spencer

Whoever is careless with the truth in small matters cannot be trusted with important matters.

—Albert Einstein

Truth must be repeated again and again, because error is constantly being preached round about.

— Johann Wolfgang von Goethe

Though the whole world would grumble, I will speak my mind.

—Cicero

We cannot possess the truth fully until it has entered into the very substance of our life by good habits and by a certain perfection of moral activity.

—Thomas Merton

I am not afraid of the pen, or the scaffold, or the sword. I will tell the truth whenever I please.

—Mary Harris "Mother" Jones

The greatest and noblest pleasure which men can have in this world is to discover new truths; and the next is to shake off old prejudices.

—Frederick the Great

Still I hope I shall always possess firmness and virtue enough to maintain (what I consider the most enviable of all titles) the character of an honest man.

—George Washington

We learned about honesty and integrity—that the truth matters, that you don't take shortcuts or play by your own set of rules, and success doesn't count unless you earn it fair and square.

—Michelle Obama

Being entirely honest with oneself is a good exercise.

—Sigmund Freud

Let's talk sense to the American people. Let's tell them the truth . . . Better we lose the election than mislead the people, and better we lose than misgovern the people.

—Adlai Stevenson

I believe that truth is the glue that holds government together. Compromise is the oil that make governments go.

—Gerald Ford

What I know for sure is that speaking your truth is the most powerful tool we all have.

—Oprah Winfrey

Let us labor for that larger and larger comprehension of truth, that more and more thorough repudiation of error, which shall make the history of mankind a series of ascending developments.

—Horace Mann

Truth is the only safe ground to stand upon.

—Elizabeth Cady Stanton

Truth is powerful and it prevails.

—Sojourner Truth

FREEDOM AND RIGHTS

I had reasoned this out in my mind; there was two things I had a right to, liberty, or death; if I could not have one, I would have the other; for no man should take me alive.

—**Harriet Tubman**

Those who deny freedom to others deserve it not for themselves.

—**Abraham Lincoln**

We realize the importance of our voices only when they are silenced.

—**Malala Yousafzai**

The supreme belief of our society is the dignity and freedom of the individual. To the respect of that dignity, to the defense of that freedom, all effort is pledged.

—**Dwight D. Eisenhower**

Those who expect to reap the blessings of freedom must, like men, undergo the fatigue of supporting it.

—**Thomas Paine**

Those men and women are fortunate who are born at a time when a great struggle for human freedom is in progress.

—**Emmeline Pankhurst**

Freedom is not simply the absence of tyranny or oppression. Nor is freedom the license to do whatever we like. Freedom has an inner "logic" which distinguishes it and ennobles it: freedom is ordered to the truth, and is fulfilled in man's quest for truth and in man's living in the truth.

—**Pope John Paul II**

The jaws of power are always opened to devour, and her arm is always stretched out, if possible, to destroy the freedom of thinking, speaking, and writing.

—**John Adams**

There are more instances of the abridgement of the freedom of the people by gradual and silent encroachments of those in power than by violent and sudden usurpation.

—**James Madison**

History teaches that grave threats to liberty often come in times of urgency, when constitutional rights seem too extravagant to endure.

—**Thurgood Marshall**

Liberty has never come from the government. Liberty has always come from the subjects of the government. The history of liberty is a history of resistance. The history of liberty is a history of the limitations of governmental power, not the increase of it.

—Woodrow Wilson

Freedom is the very essence of our economy and society. Without freedom the human mind is prevented from unleashing its creative force. But what is also clear is that this freedom does not stand alone. It is freedom in responsibility and freedom to exercise responsibility.

—Angela Merkel

Struggle is a never ending process. Freedom is never really won—you earn it and win it in every generation.

—Coretta Scott King

Freedom of the press is not an end in itself but a means to the end of achieving a free society.

—Felix Frankfurter

The liberty enjoyed by the people of these States of worshipping Almighty God, agreeably to their consciences, is not only among the choicest of their blessings, but also of their rights.

—George Washington

Freedom is not a gift bestowed upon us by other men, but a right that belongs to us by the laws of God and nature.

—**Benjamin Franklin**

I am glad to see that men are getting their rights, but I want women to get theirs, and while the water is stirring I will step into the pool.

—**Sojourner Truth**

Freedom is the last, best hope of earth.

—**Abraham Lincoln**

People tend to forget their duties but remember their rights.

—**Indira Gandhi**

Where, after all, do universal human rights begin? In small places, close to home—so close and so small that they cannot be seen on any map of the world . . . Such are the places where every man, woman, and child seeks equal justice, equal opportunity, equal dignity without discrimination. Unless these rights have meaning there, they have little meaning anywhere. Without concerted citizen action to uphold them close to home, we shall look in vain for progress in the larger world.

—**Eleanor Roosevelt**

To deny people their human rights is to challenge their very humanity.

—Nelson Mandela

In recognizing the humanity of our fellow beings, we pay ourselves the highest tribute.

—Thurgood Marshall

It means a great deal to those who are oppressed to know that they are not alone. Never let anyone tell you that what you are doing is insignificant.

—Desmond Tutu

It does not matter what country we live in, who our leaders are or even who we are. Because we are human, we therefore have rights. And because we have rights, governments are bound to protect them.

—Hillary Rodham Clinton

GOVERNMENT AND DEMOCRACY

Why has government been instituted at all? Because the passions
of men will not conform to the dictates of reason and justice
without constraint.

—Alexander Hamilton

This government, the offspring of our own choice, uninfluenced
and unawed, adopted upon full investigation and mature deliberation,
completely free in its principles, in the distribution of its powers,
uniting security with energy, and containing within itself a provision
for its own amendment, has a just claim to your confidence and
your support. Respect for its authority, compliance with its laws,
acquiescence in its measures, are duties enjoined by the fundamental
maxims of true liberty. The basis of our political systems is the right
of the people to make and to alter their constitutions of government.
But the Constitution which at any time exists, till changed by an
explicit and authentic act of the whole people, is sacredly obligatory
upon all. The very idea of the power and the right of the people
to establish government presupposes the duty of every individual
to obey the established government.

—George Washington

No Government, no Head of Government can last if the people feel that this Government is not going to defend the security of the country.

—**Indira Gandhi**

The accumulation of all powers, legislative, executive, and judiciary, in the same hands, whether of one, a few, or many, and whether hereditary, self-appointed, or elective, may justly be pronounced the very definition of tyranny.

—**James Madison**

There is danger from all men. The only maxim of a free government ought to be to trust no man living with power to endanger the public liberty.

—**John Adams**

If men were angels, no government would be necessary. If angels were to govern men, neither external nor internal controls on government would be necessary. In framing a government which is to be administered by men over men, the great difficulty lies in this: you must first enable the government to control the governed; and in the next place oblige it to control itself. A dependence on the people is, no doubt, the primary control on the government; but experience has taught mankind the necessity of auxiliary precautions.

—**James Madison**

I believe that Americans should be deeply skeptical of government power. You cannot trust people in power. The founders knew that. That's why they divided power among three branches, to set interest against interest.

—James Comey

The basis of our governments being the opinion of the people, the very first object should be to keep that right; and were it left to me to decide whether we should have a government without newspapers or newspapers without a government, I should not hesitate a moment to prefer the latter.

—Thomas Jefferson

The constant free flow of communication among us—enabling the free exchange of ideas—forms the very bloodstream of our nation. It keeps the mind and the body of our democracy eternally vital, eternally young.

—Franklin D. Roosevelt

[L]et those who are to preside over the state obey two precepts of Plato,—one, that they so watch for the well-being of their fellow-citizens that they have reference to it in whatever they do, forgetting their own private interests; the other, that they care for the whole body politic, and not, while they watch over a portion of it, neglect other portions.

—Cicero

In a democracy, dissent is an act of faith.

—**J. William Fulbright**

It has been said that democracy is the worst form of government except all those other forms that have been tried from time to time.

—**Winston Churchill**

Efficiency can never be substituted for due process. Is not a dictatorship the more "efficient" form of government?

—**Thurgood Marshall**

The experience of democracy is like the experience of life itself—always changing, infinite in its variety, sometimes turbulent and all the more valuable for having been tested by adversity.

—**Jimmy Carter**

LAW, EQUALITY, AND JUSTICE

Let every American, every lover of liberty, every well wisher to his posterity, swear by the blood of the Revolution, never to violate in the least particular, the laws of the country; and never to tolerate their violation by others.

—**Abraham Lincoln**

No man is above the law and no man is below it; nor do we ask any man's permission when we require him to obey it. Obedience to the law is demanded as a right; not asked as a favor.

—**Theodore Roosevelt**

If we desire respect for the law we must first make the law respectable.

—**Louis D. Brandeis**

Fragile as reason is and limited as law is as the institutionalized medium of reason, that's all we have standing between us and the tyranny of mere will and the cruelty of unbridled, undisciplined feeling.

—**Felix Frankfurter**

It is the spirit and not the form of law that keeps justice alive.

—**Earl Warren**

There can be no truer principle than this—that every individual of the community at large has an equal right to the protection of government.

—**Alexander Hamilton**

The great can protect themselves, but the poor and humble require the arm and shield of the law.

—**Andrew Jackson**

I am not included within the pale of this glorious anniversary! Your high independence only reveals the immeasurable distance between us. The blessings in which you, this day, rejoice, are not enjoyed in common. The rich inheritance of justice, liberty, prosperity and independence, bequeathed by your fathers, is shared by you, not by me. The sunlight that brought life and healing to you, has brought stripes and death to me. This Fourth of July is yours, not mine. You may rejoice. I must mourn.

—**Frederick Douglass**

For shame! For shame! You dare to cry out "Liberty" when you hold us in places against our will, driving us from place to place as if we were beasts.

—**Sarah Winnemucca**

Only base men and oppressors can rejoice in a triumph of injustice over the weak and defenseless, for weakness ought itself to protect from assaults of pride, prejudice, and power.

—**Frederick Douglass**

I believe the tendency of truth, on this subject, is to equalize the sexes; and that, when truth directs us, there will be no longer assumed authority on one side, or admitted inferiority on the other; but that as we advance in the cultivation of all our powers, physical as well as intellectual and moral, we shall see that our independence is equal, our dependence mutual, and our obligations reciprocal.

—**Lucretia Mott**

I never doubted that equal rights was the right direction. Most reforms, most problems are complicated. But to me there is nothing complicated about ordinary equality.

—**Alice Paul**

History will have to record that the greatest tragedy of this period of social transition was not the strident clamor of the bad people, but the appalling silence of the good people.

—**Martin Luther King, Jr.**

Justice is truth in action.

—**Benjamin Disraeli**

One hundred years of delay have passed since President Lincoln freed the slaves, yet their heirs, their grandsons, are not fully free. They are not yet freed from the bonds of injustice. They are not yet freed from social and economic oppression. And this Nation, for all its hopes and all its boasts, will not be fully free until all its citizens are free.

—**John F. Kennedy**

We have talked long enough in this country about equal rights. We have talked for a hundred years or more. It is time now to write the next chapter, and to write it in the books of law.

—**Lyndon B. Johnson**

I want you to find strength in your diversity. Let the fact that you are black or yellow or white be a source of pride and inspiration to you. Draw strength from it. Let it be someone else's problem, but never yours. Never hide behind it or use it as an excuse for not doing your best.

—**Colin Powell**

If we are to achieve a richer culture, rich in contrasting values, we must recognize the whole gamut of human potentialities, and so weave a less arbitrary social fabric, one in which each diverse human gift will find a fitting place.

—**Margaret Mead**

It's just really important that we start celebrating our differences. Let's start tolerating first, but then we need to celebrate our differences.

—**Billie Jean King**

Once people begin to see the similarities between themselves and others, instead of focusing on differences, they come to recognize that equality is essentially a matter of human rights and human dignity.

—**John Lewis**

For more than two centuries, we have strived, often at great cost, to form "a more perfect union,"—to make sure that "we, the people" applies to all the people. Many of us are only here because others fought to secure rights and opportunities for us. And we've got a responsibility to do the same for future generations.

—**Barack Obama**

Proper morals, and not force, are the bases of law; and that to practice justice is to practice liberty.

—**Simón Bolívar**

Justice is indiscriminately due to all, without regard to numbers, wealth, or rank.

—**John Jay**

Justice is conscience, not a personal conscience, but the conscience of the whole of humanity.

—**Aleksandr Solzhenitsyn**

Memories of our lives, of our works and our deeds will continue in others.

—**Rosa Parks**

Whenever a separation is made between liberty and justice, neither is, in my opinion, safe.

—**Edmund Burke**

We shall overcome because the arc of a moral universe is long, but it bends toward justice.

—**Martin Luther King, Jr.**

POLITICS AND POLITICIANS

Politics are almost as exciting as war, and quite as dangerous. In war, you can only be killed once, but in politics many times.

—Winston Churchill

I seldom think of politics more than eighteen hours a day.

—Lyndon B. Johnson

All see, and most admire, the glare which hovers round the external trappings of elevated office. To me there is nothing in it, beyond the lustre which may be reflected from its connection with a power of promoting human felicity.

—George Washington

The point is, politics has never been for the thin-skinned or the faint of heart, and if you enter the arena, you should expect to get roughed up. Moreover, Democracy in a nation of more than 300 million people is inherently difficult.

—Barack Obama

I lost the first race I ever ran, for the Cambridge City Council, by 160 votes because I took my own neighborhood for granted. My father took me aside after the election and told me, "All politics is local. Don't forget it."

—**Tip O'Neill**

That's what politics is about. It's about your opponents slinging arrows as fast and effectively as they possibly can, and your job is to block them and punch back.

—**Kirsten Gillibrand**

I always cheer up immensely if an attack is particularly wounding because I think, well, if they attack one personally, it means they have not a single political argument left.

—**Margaret Thatcher**

When the Founding Fathers arrived here in Philadelphia to forge a new nation, they didn't come as Democrats or Republicans, or to nominate a presidential candidate. They came as patriots who feared party politics. I know how they felt. I've been a Democrat, I've been a Republican, and I eventually became an independent because I don't believe either party has a monopoly on good ideas or strong leadership.

—**Michael Bloomberg**

If women could go into your Congress, I think justice would soon be done to the Indians.

—**Sarah Winnemucca**

I recognize the Republican party as the sheet anchor of the colored man's political hopes and the ark of his safety.

—**Frederick Douglass**

Men often oppose a thing merely because they have had no agency in planning it, or because it may have been planned by those whom they dislike.

—**Alexander Hamilton**

Standing in the middle of the road is very dangerous; you get knocked down by traffic from both sides.

—**Margaret Thatcher**

The people to fear are not those who disagree with you, but those who disagree with you and are too cowardly to let you know.

—**Napoleon Bonaparte**

It was my fortune, or misfortune, to be called to the office of the Chief Executive without any previous political training.

—**Ulysses S. Grant**

Every man who takes office in Washington either grows or swells, and when I give a man an office, I watch him carefully to see whether he is growing or swelling.

—Woodrow Wilson

The White House isn't the place to learn how to deal with international crisis, the balance of power, war and peace, and the economic future of the next generation.

—Joe Biden

Extremism in the pursuit of the Presidency is an unpardonable vice. Moderation in the affairs of the nation is the highest virtue.

—Lyndon B. Johnson

The biggest problem in Washington is the lack of empathy. The fact that too many members of Congress, too many senators, cannot live a day in someone else's shoes. And don't even want to.

—Kirsten Gillibrand

My experience is that a number of the men I have dealt with in politics demonstrate precisely those characteristics which they attribute to women—vanity and an inability to make decisions.

—Margaret Thatcher

What I find is with all due deference to—deference to our male colleagues, that women's styles tend to be more collaborative.

—Susan Collins

Any man who has had the job I've had and didn't have a sense of humor wouldn't still be here.

—Harry S. Truman

If you do politics the right way, I believe, you can actually make people's lives better. And integrity is the minimum ante to get into the game.

—Joe Biden

AMERICA

Yesterday the greatest question was decided which was ever debated in America; and a greater perhaps never was, nor will be, decided upon men. A resolution was passed without one dissenting colony, that those United Colonies are, and of right ought to be, free and independent states.

—**John Adams**

We hold these truths to be self-evident; that all men are created equal; that they are endowed by their creator with certain unalienable rights; that among these are life, liberty, and the pursuit of happiness.

—**Thomas Jefferson**

The welfare of our country is the great object to which our cares and efforts ought to be directed—And I shall derive great satisfaction from cooperation with you, in the pleasing though arduous task of ensuring to our fellow citizens the blessings which they have a right to expect from a free and equal government.

—**George Washington**

What charms me [in America] is that all citizens are brethren.

—**Marquis de Lafayette**

I walk on untrodden ground. There is scarcely any part of my conduct which may not hereafter be drawn into precedent.

—**George Washington**

The life of the nation is secure only while the nation is honest, truthful, and virtuous.

—**Frederick Douglass**

Our country offers the most wonderful example of democratic government on a giant scale that the world has ever seen; and the peoples of the world are watching to see whether we succeed or fail.

—**Theodore Roosevelt**

The strength of our Nation must continue to be used in the interest of all our people rather than a privileged few. It must continue to be used unselfishly in the struggle for world peace and the betterment of mankind.

—**Harry S. Truman**

And so, my fellow Americans: ask not what your country can do for you—ask what you can do for your country. My fellow citizens of the world: ask not what America will do for you, but what together we can do for the freedom of man.

—**John F. Kennedy**

Some may try and tell us that this is the end of an era. But what they overlook is that in America, every day is a new beginning, and every sunset is merely the latest milestone on a voyage that never ends. For this is the land that has never become, but is always in the act of becoming. Emerson was right: America is the Land of Tomorrow.

—**Ronald Reagan**

At the beginning of the World Series of 1947, I experienced a completely new emotion when the National Anthem was played. This time, I thought, it is being played for me, as much as for anyone else. This is organized major league baseball, and I am standing here with all the others, and everything that takes place includes me.

—**Jackie Robinson**

I am America. I am the part you won't recognize. But get used to me. Black, confident, cocky; my name, not yours; my religion, not yours; my goals, my own; get used to me.

—**Muhammad Ali**

Give me your tired, your poor,
Your huddled masses yearning to breathe free,
The wretched refuse of your teeming shore.
Send these, the homeless, tempest-tossed, to me,
I lift my lamp beside the golden door.

—**Emma Lazarus**

When I look out at this convention, I see the face of America, red, yellow, brown, black, and white. We are all precious in God's sight—the real rainbow coalition.

—**Jesse Jackson**

Our attitude towards immigration reflects our faith in the American ideal. We have always believed it possible for men and women who start at the bottom to rise as far as their talent and energy allow. Neither race nor place of birth should affect their chances.

—**Robert F. Kennedy**

More than any other nation on Earth, America has constantly drawn strength and spirit from wave after wave of immigrants. In each generation, they have proved to be the most restless, the most adventurous, the most innovative, the most industrious of people. Bearing different memories, honoring different heritages, they have strengthened our economy, enriched our culture, renewed our promise of freedom and opportunity for all.

—**Bill Clinton**

And let me offer lesson number one about America: All great change in America begins at the dinner table. So, tomorrow night in the kitchen I hope the talking begins. And children, if your parents haven't been teaching you what it means to be an American, let 'em know and nail 'em on it. That would be a very American thing to do.

—**Ronald Reagan**

I am the proud daughter of Indian immigrants who reminded my brothers, my sister and me every single day how blessed we were to live in this country. They loved the fact that only in America, we could be as successful as we wanted to be, and nothing would stand in our way.

—**Nikki Haley**

We need comprehensive immigration reform. Dr. King wouldn't be pleased at all to know that there are millions of people living in the shadow, living in fear in places like Georgia and Alabama.

—**John Lewis**

You grow up in America and you're told from day one, "This is the land of opportunity." That everybody has an equal chance to make it in this country. And then you look at places like Harlem, and you say, "That is absolutely a lie."

—**Geoffrey Canada**

The essence of America—that which really unites us—is not ethnicity, or nationality or religion—it is an idea—and what an idea it is: That you can come from humble circumstances and do great things. That it doesn't matter where you came from but where you are going.

—**Condoleezza Rice**

There is nothing wrong with America that cannot be fixed by what is right with America.

—**Bill Clinton**

What a privilege it is to serve this big, boisterous, brawling, intemperate, striving, daring, beautiful, bountiful, brave, magnificent country. With all our flaws, all our mistakes, with all the frailties of human nature as much on display as our virtues, with all the rancor and anger of our politics, we are blessed.

—**John McCain**

Americans are fighters. We're tough, resourceful and creative, and if we have the chance to fight on a level playing field, where everyone pays a fair share and everyone has a real shot, then no one—no one can stop us.

—**Elizabeth Warren**

My fellow Americans, we cannot be seduced into cynicism about our politics, because cynicism is a refuge for cowards and this nation is and must always be the home of the brave. We are the United States of America. We will not falter or fail. We will not retreat or surrender— we will not surrender our values, we will not surrender our ideals, we will not surrender the moral high ground.

—**Cory Booker**

Let us keep our eyes on the issues and work for the things we all believe in. Let each of us put our country ahead of our party, and ahead of our own personal interests.

—**Harry S. Truman**

That's the America I know. That's the country we love. Clear-eyed. Big-hearted. Undaunted by challenge. Optimistic that unarmed truth and unconditional love will have the final word. That's what makes me so hopeful about our future. I believe in change because I believe in you, the American people.

—**Barack Obama**

—————

Our dignity, our character, our rights have all been under attack, and a platform of hate and division assumed power yesterday. But the president is not America. His cabinet is not America. Congress is not America. We are America. And we are here to stay.

—**America Ferrera**

—————

We didn't crumble after 9/11. We didn't falter after the Boston Marathon. But we're America. Americans will never, ever stand down. We endure. We overcome. We own the finish line.

—**Joe Biden**

—————

The American dream belongs to all of us.

—**Kamala Harris**

—————

Our American heritage is threatened as much by our own indifference as it is by the most unscrupulous office or by the most powerful foreign threat. The future of this republic is in the hands of the American voter.

—**Dwight D. Eisenhower**

To fear the world we have organized and led for three-quarters of a century, to abandon the ideals we have advanced around the globe, to refuse the obligations of international leadership and our duty to remain "the last best hope of earth" for the sake of some half-baked, spurious nationalism cooked up by people who would rather find scapegoats than solve problems is as unpatriotic as an attachment to any other tired dogma of the past that Americans consigned to the ash heap of history.

—**John McCain**

It's not the hand that signs the laws that holds the destiny of America. It's the hand that casts the ballot.

—**Harry S. Truman**

We must rekindle the fire of idealism in our society, for nothing suffocates the promise of America more than unbounded cynicism and indifference.

—**Joe Biden**

For all my years in public life, I have believed that America must sail toward the shores of liberty and justice for all. There is no end to that journey, only the next great voyage. We know the future will outlast all of us, but I believe that all of us will live on in the future we make.

—**Ted Kennedy**

ACTIVISM AND REFORM

Organize, agitate, educate, must be our war cry.

—Susan B. Anthony

We are here, not because we are law-breakers; we are here in our efforts to become law-makers.

—Emmeline Pankhurst

When a just cause reaches its flood tide, whatever stands in the way must fall before its overwhelming power.

—Carrie Chapman Catt

I want you to pledge yourselves in the convention to stand as one solid army against the foes of human labor. Think of the thousands who are killed every year and there is no redress for it. We will fight until the mines are made secure and human life valued more than props. Look things in the face. Don't fear a governor; don't fear anybody. You pay the governor; he has a right to protect you. You are the biggest part of the population in the state. You create its wealth, so I say, "Let the fight go on; if nobody else will keep on, I will."

—Mary Harris "Mother" Jones

Cautious, careful people, always casting about to preserve their reputations can never effect a reform.

—**Susan B. Anthony**

The most potent weapon in the hands of the oppressor is the mind of the oppressed.

—**Stephen Biko**

We didn't have any of what they called Civil Rights back then. It was just a matter of survival—existing from day to day.

—**Rosa Parks**

If we simply accept and acquiesce in the face of discrimination, we accept the responsibility ourselves and allow those responsible to salve their conscience by believing that they have our acceptance and concurrence. We should, therefore, protest openly everything in the newspapers, on the radio, in the movies that smacks of discrimination or slander.

—**Mary McLeod Bethune**

The revolution is at hand, and we must free ourselves of the chains of political and economic slavery. . . . We cannot be patient, we do not want to be free gradually. We want our freedom, and we want it now.

—**John Lewis**

Now is the time to make real the promises of democracy.

—**Martin Luther King, Jr.**

<hr/>

While I had been fighting in Vietnam alongside brave soldiers trying to preserve their freedom, in my own land a long-simmering conflict had turned into an open fight in our streets and cities—a fight that had to be won.

—**Colin Powell**

<hr/>

Silence becomes cowardice when occasion demands speaking out the whole truth and acting accordingly.

—**Mahatma Gandhi**

<hr/>

There may be times when we are powerless to prevent injustice, but there must never be a time when we fail to protest.

—**Elie Wiesel**

<hr/>

Those of us who shout the loudest about Americanism in making character assassinations are all too frequently those who, by our own words and acts, ignore some of the basic principles of Americanism: the right to criticize; the right to hold unpopular beliefs; the right to protest; the right of independent thought.

—**Margaret Chase Smith**

We have said from the very beginning that our movement is about. . . . the fact that there isn't much quality of life for black people in this country. Our conditions are pretty similar to conditions for black people around the world, which is how we know that it's not isolated—that it's intentional and that it's systematic.

—**Alicia Garza**

I am not looking for approval. I have to stand up for people that are oppressed. If they take football away, my endorsements from me, I know that I stood up for what is right.

—**Colin Kaepernick**

Nonviolent protest is important and has always been to advancing our nation. And for Muhammad Ali to artists and entertainers who participated in movements from the women's rights movement to the civil rights movement, this is a noble tradition in our country.

—**Cory Booker**

All of us in law enforcement must be honest enough to acknowledge that much of our history is not pretty. At many points in American history, law enforcement enforced the status quo, a status quo that was often brutally unfair to disfavored groups.

—**James Comey**

The struggle is eternal. The tribe increases. Somebody else carries on.

—**Ella J. Baker**

The Women's March was the biggest single protest in American history. Hundreds of thousands of people gathered in cities like New York, Los Angeles, and Chicago. Thousands also turned out in places like Wyoming and Alaska. In Washington, the march dwarfed the crowd that gathered to see Trump's inauguration the day before. And it was completely peaceful. Maybe that's what happens when you put women in charge.

—**Hillary Rodham Clinton**

If I can symbolize the ability to pursue gender equality, racial equality, and to be truthful about our experiences, then, absolutely, that's what I want to be.

—**Anita Hill**

#MeToo is essentially about survivors supporting survivors. And it's really about community healing and community action. Although we can't define what healing looks like for people, we can set the stage and give people the resources to have access to healing. And that means legitimate things like policies and laws that change that support survivors.

—**Tarana Burke**

I think what we are experiencing now is a tectonic shift underneath our feet, where women and men are feeling that we can no longer not say the truth. And when the truth is said, there is maybe a ripple in our culture right now that is going to allow for there to be a change.

—**America Ferrera**

So I want all the girls watching here, now, to know that a new day is on the horizon! And when that new day finally dawns, it will be because of a lot of magnificent women, many of whom are right here in this room tonight, and some pretty phenomenal men, fighting hard to make sure that they become the leaders who take us to the time when nobody ever has to say "Me too" again.

—**Oprah Winfrey**

How many more mothers? How many more fathers need to shed tears of grief before we do something? Give us a vote. Let us vote. We came here to do our job. We came here to work.

—**John Lewis**

Now, I'm not naive. I have spoken at too many memorials during the course of this presidency. I've hugged too many families who have lost a loved one to senseless violence. And I've seen how a spirit of unity, born of tragedy, can gradually dissipate, overtaken by the return to business as usual, by inertia and old habits and expediency.

—**Barack Obama**

We need enthusiasm, imagination and the ability to face facts, even unpleasant ones, bravely. We need to correct, by drastic means if necessary, the faults in our economic system from which we now suffer. We need the courage of the young.

—**Franklin D. Roosevelt**

One of the great liabilities of history is that all too many people fail to remain awake through great periods of social change. Every society has its protectors of status quo and its fraternities of the indifferent who are notorious for sleeping through revolutions. Today, our very survival depends on our ability to stay awake, to adjust to new ideas, to remain vigilant and to face the challenge of change.

—**Martin Luther King, Jr.**

We face, therefore, a moral crisis as a country and a people. It cannot be met by repressive police action. It cannot be left to increased demonstrations in the streets. It cannot be quieted by token moves or talk. It is a time to act in the Congress, in your State and local legislative body and, above all, in all of our daily lives. It is not enough to pin the blame on others, to say this a problem of one section of the country or another or deplore the facts that we face. A great change is at hand, and our task, our obligation, is to make that revolution, that change, peaceful and constructive for all. Those who do nothing are inviting shame, as well as violence. Those who act boldly are recognizing right, as well as reality.

—**John F. Kennedy**

We must stand together; if we don't, there will be no victory for any one of us.

—**Mary Harris "Mother" Jones**

You must never, ever give up. You must never, ever give in. You must never, ever give out. We must keep the faith because we are one people. We are brothers and sisters. We all live in the same house: The American house.

—**John Lewis**

WOMEN

I declare to you that woman must not depend upon the protection of man, but must be taught to protect herself, and there I take my stand.

—**Susan B. Anthony**

It took me quite a long time to develop a voice, and now that I have it, I am not going to be silent.

—**Madeleine Albright**

I have chosen to no longer be apologetic for my femininity. And I want to be respected in all my femaleness.

—**Chimamanda Ngozi Adichie**

Please know that I am aware of the hazards. I want to do it because I want to do it. Women must try to do things as men have tried. When they fail, their failure must be but a challenge to others.

—**Amelia Earhart**

Surround yourself with only people who are going to lift you higher.

—**Oprah Winfrey**

You could certainly say that I've never underestimated myself. There's nothing wrong with being ambitious.

—Angela Merkel

Women are leaders everywhere you look—from the CEO who runs a Fortune 500 company to the housewife who raises her children and heads her household. Our country was built by strong women, and we will continue to break down walls and defy stereotypes.

—Nancy Pelosi

I may sometimes be willing to teach for nothing, but if paid at all, I shall never do a man's work for less than a man's pay.

—Clara Barton

There is no war on women. Women are doing well. But women are thoughtful. And what we in the Republican Party and across the country, Republican, Independents and Democrat women say is we're more thoughtful than a label. We care about jobs and the economy and healthcare and education. We care about a lot of different things.

—Nikki Haley

I've always believed that one woman's success can only help another woman's success.

—Gloria Vanderbilt

We need women at all levels, including the top, to change the dynamic, reshape the conversation, to make sure women's voices are heard and heeded, not overlooked and ignored.

—**Sheryl Sandberg**

No country can ever truly flourish if it stifles the potential of its women and deprives itself of the contributions of half its citizens.

—**Michelle Obama**

Women will have achieved true equality when men share with them the responsibility of bringing up the next generation.

—**Ruth Bader Ginsburg**

Women and girls should be able to determine their own future, no matter where they're born.

—**Melinda Gates**

And to all the little girls who are watching this, never doubt that you are valuable and powerful and deserving of every chance and opportunity in the world to pursue and achieve your own dreams.

—**Hillary Rodham Clinton**

For what is done or learned by one class of women becomes, by virtue of their common womanhood, the property of all women.

—**Elizabeth Blackwell**

I was raised to be an independent woman, not the victim of anything.

—**Kamala Harris**

I raise up my voice not so I can shout, but so that those without a voice can be heard. We cannot succeed when half of us are held back.

—**Malala Yousafzai**

PEACE, WAR, AND
FOREIGN POLICY

I rejoiced at the return of peace. We are now friends with England and with all mankind. I hope it will be lasting, and that mankind will at length, as they call themselves reasonable creatures, have reason and sense enough to settle their differences without cutting throats. May we never see another war! For in my opinion there was never a good war or a bad peace.

—Benjamin Franklin

There is nothing so likely to produce peace as to be well prepared to meet an enemy.

—George Washington

True peace is not merely the absence of tension; it is the presence of justice.

—Martin Luther King, Jr.

You can't separate peace from freedom because no one can be at peace unless he has his freedom.

—Malcolm X

Peace involves work, it is not about staying calm and doing nothing. No! True peace means working so that everyone has a solution to the problems, to the needs, that they have in their homeland, in their family, in their society.

—**Pope Francis**

Peace we want because there is another war to fight against poverty, disease and ignorance. We have promises to keep to our people of work, food, clothing, and shelter, health and education.

—**Indira Gandhi**

Peace can only last where human rights are respected, where the people are fed, and where individuals and nations are free.

—**Dalai Lama**

War, in one form or another, appeared with the first man. At the dawn of history, its morality was not questioned; it was simply a fact, like drought or disease—the manner in which tribes and then civilizations sought power and settled their differences.

—**Barack Obama**

Stand firm; for well you know that hardship and danger are the price of glory, and that sweet is the savour of a life of courage and of deathless renown beyond the grave.

—**Alexander the Great**

So strong is this propensity of mankind to fall into mutual animosities, that where no substantial occasion presents itself, the most frivolous and fanciful distinctions have been sufficient to kindle their unfriendly passions and excite their most violent conflicts.

—James Madison

I know I have the body of a weak and feeble woman, but I have the heart and stomach of a king, and of a king of England too, and think foul scorn that Parma or Spain, or any prince of Europe, should dare to invade the borders of my realm. . . .

—Queen Elizabeth I

Discipline is the soul of an army. It makes small numbers formidable; procures success to the weak, and esteem to all.

—George Washington

One of the primary purposes of discipline is to produce alertness. A man who is so lethargic that he fails to salute will fall an easy victim to the enemy.

—George S. Patton

This conflict is one thing I've been waiting for. I'm well and strong and young—young enough to go to the front. If I can't be a soldier, I'll help soldiers.

—Clara Barton

My first wish would be that my military family, and the whole Army, should consider themselves as a band of brothers, willing and ready to die for each other.

—George Washington

You must do your damnedest and win . . . Never stop until you have gained the top or a grave.

—George S. Patton

March swiftly to revenge the dead, to give life to the dying, to free the oppressed, and to give liberty to all.

—Simón Bolívar

How great should be the incorruptibility of generals, how great their self-restraint in all things! How great their good faith, their affability, their natural faculties, their human touch!

—Cicero

War must be carried on systematically, and to do it you must have men of character activated by principles of honor.

—George Washington

If you start to take Vienna, take Vienna.

—Napoleon Bonaparte

Even now we can draw back—but once we cross that little bridge, we must settle things by the sword.

—**Julius Caesar**

Optimism and pessimism are infectious and they spread more rapidly from the head downward than in any other direction. . . . I firmly determined that my mannerisms and speech in public would always reflect the cheerful certainly of victory—that any pessimism and discouragement I might ever feel would be reserved for my pillow.

—**Dwight D. Eisenhower**

What is our aim? . . . Victory, victory at all costs, victory in spite of all terror; victory, however long and hard the road may be; for without victory, there is no survival.

—**Winston Churchill**

Anyone who has looked into the glazed eyes of a soldier dying on the battlefield will think hard before starting a war.

—**Otto von Bismarck**

All men are timid on entering any fight. Whether it is the first fight or the last fight, all of us are timid. Cowards are those who let their timidity get the better of their manhood.

—**George S. Patton**

Women who stepped up were measured as citizens of the nation, not as women . . . This was a people's war, and everyone was in it.

—Oveta Culp Hobby

Today we feel what Franklin Roosevelt called the warm courage of national unity. This unity against terror is now extending across the world.

—George W. Bush

This is not a battle between the United States and terrorism, but between the free and democratic world and terrorism. We therefore here in Britain stand shoulder to shoulder with our American friends in this hour of tragedy and we, like them, will not rest until this evil is driven from our world.

—Tony Blair

We have grasped the mystery of the atom and rejected the Sermon on the Mount. The world has achieved brilliance with conscience. Ours is a world of nuclear giants and ethical infants. We know more about war than we know about peace, more about killing than we know about living.

—Omar Bradley

To avoid entangling alliances has been a maxim of our policy ever since the days of Washington, and its wisdom no one will attempt to dispute.

—James Buchanan

The strongest response to terrorists is to carry on living our lives and our values as we have until now—self-confident and free, considerate and engaged. We Europeans will show our free life is stronger than any terror.

—Angela Merkel

Excessive partiality for one foreign nation and excessive dislike of another cause those whom they actuate to see danger only on one side, and serve to veil and even second the arts of influence on the other. Real patriots who may resist the intrigues of the favorite are liable to become suspected and odious, while its tools and dupes usurp the applause and confidence of the people, to surrender their interests.

—George Washington

Praise from enemies is suspicious; it cannot flatter an honorable man unless it is given after the cessation of hostilities.

—Napoleon Bonaparte

Human rights is the soul of our foreign policy. And I say this with assurance, because human rights is the very soul of our sense of nationhood.

—**Jimmy Carter**

The United States can't solve all of the problems in the world. But the problems in the world can't be solved without the United States. And therefore, we have to husband our resources, among which is this incredibly valuable asset of global leadership, and figure out how we can best deploy it.

—**Hillary Rodham Clinton**

HAPPINESS, SUCCESS,
AND ACHIEVEMENT

The consideration that human happiness and moral duty are inseparably connected will always continue to prompt me to promote the former by inculcating the practice of the latter.

—**George Washington**

Human felicity is produced not so much by great pieces of good fortune that seldom happen, as by little advantages that occur every day.

—**Benjamin Franklin**

I have also learned from experience that the greater part of our happiness or misery depends on our dispositions, and not on our circumstances.

—**Martha Washington**

Do the best you can in every task, no matter how unimportant it may seem at the time. No one learns more about a problem than the person at the bottom.

—**Sandra Day O'Connor**

Happiness is when what you think, what you say, and what you do are in harmony.

—**Mahatma Gandhi**

Be happy in the moment, that's enough. Each moment is all we need, not more.

—**Mother Teresa**

Make the most of yourself by fanning the tiny, inner sparks of possibility into flames of achievement.

—**Golda Meir**

Seek out people to work with who are brimming with talent, energy, integrity, optimism, and generosity.

—**Martha Stewart**

It is the ultimate luxury to combine passion and contribution. It's also a very clear path to happiness.

—**Sheryl Sandberg**

I was taught that the way of progress is neither swift nor easy.

—**Marie Curie**

Success is to be measured not so much by the position that one has reached in life as by the obstacles which he has overcome while trying to succeed.

—Booker T. Washington

People become really quite remarkable when they start thinking that they can do things. When they believe in themselves they have the first secret of success.

—Norman Vincent Peale

Whatever the job you are asked to do at whatever level, do a good job because your reputation is your résumé.

—Madeleine Albright

I studied the lives of great men and famous women; and I have found that the men and women who got to the top were those who did the jobs they had in hand, with everything they had of energy and enthusiasm and hard work.

—Harry S. Truman

I have spent most of my life studying the lives of other peoples, faraway peoples, so that Americans might better understand themselves.

—Margaret Mead

I always tell young people, "go ahead and do it. You can apologize later."

—**Grace Hopper**

Only those who dare to fail greatly can ever achieve greatly.

—**Robert F. Kennedy**

Never work just for money or for power. They won't save your soul or help you sleep at night.

—**Marian Wright Edelman**

Life is full of surprises and serendipity. Being open to unexpected turns in the road is an important part of success.

—**Condoleezza Rice**

You know you're a success when you look at your kids and realize they turned out better than you.

—**Joe Biden**

The secret of success in life is for a man to be ready for his opportunity when it comes.

—**Benjamin Disraeli**

Try not to become a man of success, but rather a man of value.

—**Albert Einstein**

With audacity one can undertake anything.

—**Napoleon Bonaparte**

I've hit 755 home runs, and I did it without putting a needle in my arm or a whiskey bottle in my mouth.

—**Hank Aaron**

Natural talent only determines the limits of your athletic potential. It's dedication and a willingness to discipline your life that makes you great.

—**Billie Jean King**

One important key to success is self-confidence. An important key to self-confidence is preparation.

—**Arthur Ashe**

There are no secrets to success. It is the result of preparation, hard work and learning from failure.

—**Colin Powell**

Don't let complexity stop you. Be activists. Take on the big inequities. It will be one of the great experiences of your lives.

—**Bill Gates**

To love what you do and feel that it matters—how could anything be more fun?

—**Katharine Graham**

RELIGION, MORALITY, CHARACTER, AND VIRTUE

I have felt his hand upon me in great trials and submitted to his guidance, and I trust that as he shall further open the way, I will be ready to walk therein, relying on his help and trusting in his goodness and wisdom.

—**Abraham Lincoln**

That is the religious experience: the astonishment of meeting someone who is waiting for you.

—**Pope Francis**

When we come to the end of ourselves, we come to the beginning of God.

—**Billy Graham**

Religion to me is simply the conviction that all human beings must hold some belief in a power greater than themselves, and that whatever their religious belief may be, it must move them to live better in this world and to approach whatever the future holds with serenity.

—**Eleanor Roosevelt**

I have been privileged to meet some of our world's great religious leaders, among them Roman Catholic, Protestant, and Orthodox Christians, Jews, Muslims, and Buddhists. Despite their profound differences, each speaks from a deep wellspring of love that affirms life and yearns for men and women to open their hearts like children to God and one another.

—**Hillary Rodham Clinton**

Just to be is a blessing. Just to live is holy.

—**Abraham Joshua Heschel**

This is my simple religion. There is no need for temples; no need for complicated philosophy. Our own brain, our own heart is our temple; the philosophy is kindness.

—**Dalai Lama**

All religions must be tolerated and the sole concern of officials is to ensure that one denomination does not interfere with another, for here everyone can seek salvation in the manner that seems best to him.

—**Frederick the Great**

Every man, conducting himself as a good citizen, and being accountable to God alone for his religious opinions, ought to be protected in worshipping the Deity according to the dictates of his own conscience.

—**George Washington**

Over the years my religion has changed and my spirituality has evolved. Religion and spirituality are very different, but people often confuse the two. Some things cannot be taught, but they can be awakened in the heart. Spirituality is recognizing the divine light that is within us all. It doesn't belong to any particular religion; it belongs to everyone.

—**Muhammad Ali**

Any religion that professes to be concerned with the souls of men and is not concerned with the slums that damn them, and the social conditions that cripple them is a dry-as-dust religion.

—**Martin Luther King, Jr.**

The act of acting morally is behaving as if everything we do matters.

—**Gloria Steinem**

My character and good name are in my own keeping. Life with disgrace is dreadful. A glorious death is to be envied.

—**Horatio Nelson**

Character is far more important than intellect in making a man a good citizen or successful at his calling—meaning by character not only such qualities as honesty and truthfulness, but courage, perseverance, and self-reliance.

—**Theodore Roosevelt**

You can easily judge the character of others by how they treat those who can do nothing for them or to them.

—**Malcolm S. Forbes**

Character is a by-product; it is produced in the great manufacture of daily duty.

—**Woodrow Wilson**

Humility is the foundation of all the other virtues hence, in the soul in which this virtue does not exist there cannot be any other virtue except in mere appearance.

—**St. Augustine of Hippo**

Humility must always be doing its work like a bee making its honey in the hive: without humility all will be lost.

—**St. Teresa of Ávila**

My parents . . . never stopped reminding me that my blessings sprang from countless ordinary Americans who had shown extraordinary acts of kindness and decency. . . . I was told that we can't pay those Americans back for their colossal acts of service, but we have an obligation to pay it forward to others through our service and sacrifice.

—**Cory Booker**

We learned about gratitude and humility—that so many people had a hand in our success, from the teachers who inspired us to the janitors who kept our school clean. . . . and we were taught to value everyone's contribution and treat everyone with respect.

—**Michelle Obama**

Labor to keep alive in your breast that little spark of celestial fire called conscience.

—**George Washington**

One thing that I ask of you: Never be afraid of giving. There is a deep joy in giving, since what we receive is much more than what we give.

—**Mother Teresa**

Carry out a random act of kindness, with no expectation of reward, safe in the knowledge that one day someone might do the same for you.

—**Princess Diana**

A life isn't significant except for its impact on others' lives.

—**Jackie Robinson**

Darkness cannot drive our darkness; only light can do that. Hate cannot drive our hate; only love can do that.

—**Martin Luther King, Jr.**

Virtue alone is sufficient to make a man great, glorious and happy.

—**Benjamin Franklin**

Love and compassion are necessities, not luxuries. Without them, humanity cannot survive.

—**Dalai Lama**

Tolerance and compassion are active, not passive states, born of the capacity to listen, to observe and to respect others.

—**Indira Gandhi**

My humanity is bound up in yours for we can only be human together.

—**Desmond Tutu**

FAMILY, FRIENDSHIP, AND LIFE'S PLEASURES

All that I am, or hope to be, I owe to my angel mother.

—Abraham Lincoln

I do not recollect of ever seeing my mother by the light of day. She would lie down with me and get me to sleep, but long before I waked she was gone.

—Frederick Douglass

My mother was the making of me. She was so true and so sure of me, I felt that I had someone to live for—someone I must not disappoint. The memory of my mother will always be a blessing to me.

—Thomas Edison

From my father I learned mildness, tranquil constancy in decisions taken after close examination, lack of vain conceit in so-called honors, a love of hard work, and endurance.

—Marcus Aurelius

My father, Theodore Roosevelt, was the best man I ever knew. He combined strength and courage with gentleness, tenderness, and great unselfishness.

—**Theodore Roosevelt**

My father was a feminist from the day I was born; there was nothing his little girl couldn't do. And he modeled that in his relationship with my mother.

—**Condoleezza Rice**

As much as I converse with sages and heroes, they have very little of my love or admiration. I long for rural and domestic scenes, for the warbling of birds and the prattle of my children.

—**John Adams**

I have found the best way to give advice to your children is to find out what they want and then advise them to do it.

—**Harry S. Truman**

It is my pleasure that my children are free and happy, and unrestrained by parental tyranny. Love is the chain whereby to bind a child to its parents.

—**Abraham Lincoln**

I live for my sons. I would be lost without them.

—**Princess Diana**

For unflagging interest and enjoyment, a household of children, if things go reasonably well, certainly makes all other forms of success and achievement lose their importance by comparison.

—**Theodore Roosevelt**

Though motherhood is the most important of all professions— requiring more knowledge than any other department in human affairs—there was no attention given to preparation for this office.

—**Elizabeth Cady Stanton**

Mothers are the most instinctive philosophers.

—**Harriet Beecher Stowe**

If you bungle raising your children, I don't think whatever else you do well matters very much.

—**Jacqueline Kennedy Onassis**

Parenthood changes one's world. It's almost like a switch gets flipped inside of you, and you can feel a whole new range of feelings that you never thought you'd have.

—**Steve Jobs**

Trust yourself, you know more than you think you do.

—**Dr. Benjamin Spock**

At work, you think of the children you've left at home. At home, you think of the work you've left unfinished. Such a struggle is unleashed within yourself; your heart is rent.

—**Golda Meir**

Parenthood isn't just a women's issue. It's an economic issue and an issue that affects all parents—men and women alike. As tough as juggling the demands of motherhood and being a senator can be, I'm hardly alone or unique as a working parent.

—**Tammy Duckworth**

Boys want to grow up to be like their male role models. And boys who grow up in homes with absent fathers search the hardest to figure out what it means to be male.

—**Geoffrey Canada**

Sometimes people can hunger for more than bread. It is possible that our children, our husband, our wife, do not hunger for bread, do not need clothes, do not lack a house. But are we equally sure that none of them feels alone, abandoned, neglected, needing some affection? That, too, is poverty.

—**Mother Teresa**

I have spent many hours of my life giving speeches and expressing my opinions. But it is almost impossible for me to express fully how deeply I love Nancy and how much she has filled my life.

—**Ronald Reagan**

I would say that the surest measure of a man's or a woman's maturity is the harmony, style, joy, and dignity he creates in his marriage, and the pleasure and inspiration he provides for his spouse.

—**Dr. Benjamin Spock**

Only two things are necessary to keep one's wife happy. One is to let her think she is having her own way, and the other, to let her have it.

—**Lyndon B. Johnson**

One of the oldest human needs is having someone to wonder where you are when you don't come home at night.

—**Margaret Mead**

There's only one thing we can be sure of, and that is the love that we have—for our children, for our families, for each other. The warmth of a small child's embrace—that is true. The memories we have of them, the joy that they bring, the wonder we see through their eyes, that fierce and boundless love we feel for them, a love that takes us out of ourselves, and binds us to something larger—we know that's what matters.

—**Barack Obama**

Friendship is the source of the greatest pleasures, and without friends even the most agreeable pursuits become tedious.

—**St. Thomas Aquinas**

Actions, not words, are the true criterion of the attachment of friends.

—**George Washington**

The influence of each human being on others in this life is a kind of immortality.

—**John Quincy Adams**

Be courteous to all, but intimate with few, and let those few be well tried before you give them your confidence.

—**George Washington**

You can make more friends in two months by becoming interested in other people than you can in two years by trying to get other people interested in you.

—**Dale Carnegie**

There is no more precious experience in life than friendship. And I am not forgetting love and marriage as I write this; the lovers, or the man and wife, who are not friends are but weakly joined together.

—**Eleanor Roosevelt**

I've been supported by a wonderful group of friends my entire adult life, and that's what really matters. They share my joys, they share my sorrows, they are with me and so understand that life is not just about the public part of your experience.

—Hillary Rodham Clinton

Lots of people want to ride with you in the limo, but what you want is someone who will take the bus with you when the limo breaks down.

—Oprah Winfrey

The friend of my adversity I shall always cherish most. I can better trust those who helped to relieve the gloom of my dark hours than those who are so ready to enjoy with me the sunshine of my prosperity.

—Ulysses S. Grant

I have friends in overalls whose friendship I would not swap for the favor of the kings of the world.

—Thomas Edison

It is that unoccupied space which makes a room habitable, as it is our leisure hours which make life endurable.

—Lin Yutang

To add a library to a house is to give that house a soul.

—Cicero

If you cannot read all your books, at any rate handle, or as it were, fondle them—peer into them, let them fall open where they will, read from the first sentence that arrests the eye, set them back on their shelves with your own hands, arrange them on your own plan so that if you do not know what is in them, you at least know where they are. Let them be your friends, let them at any rate be your acquaintances.

—Winston Churchill

Taking the time to read to children is not only a worthwhile investment but also a wonderful experience. I have visited 119 schools in Maine, and these visits are among the most rewarding experiences in my career in public service.

—Susan Collins

When power leads man toward arrogance, poetry reminds him of his limitations. When power narrows the areas of man's concern, poetry reminds him of the richness and diversity of his existence. When power corrupts, poetry cleanses. For art establishes the basic human truths which must serve as the touchstone of our judgment.

—John F. Kennedy

I have loved to cook since I was a child in my mother's kitchen. If I don't have time to cook, I'll just read a cookbook.

—Kamala Harris

A good traveler has no fixed plans and is not intent on arriving.

—**Lao Tzu**

Like all great travelers, I have seen more than I remember, and remember more than I have seen.

—**Benjamin Disraeli**

The President has warned that we are becoming a nation of spectators rather than partakers. If our added leisure means watching baseball and football on television, with no real occupation in which we put our own brains and energies to work, then I must join the President in his exhortation to begin to do things, not just watch things being done.

—**Eleanor Roosevelt**

My love of football started with my father. . . . He had wanted me to be his "All-American linebacker," and had I been a son instead of a daughter, I think I might have done it.

—**Condoleezza Rice**

When you play, play hard. When you work, don't play at all.

—**Theodore Roosevelt**

HARDSHIP, ADVERSITY, AND HOPE

This great nation will endure as it has endured, will revive and will prosper. So, first of all, let me assert my firm belief that the only thing we have to fear is fear itself—nameless, unreasoning, unjustified terror which paralyzes needed efforts to convert retreat into advance.

— **Franklin D. Roosevelt**

We shall draw from the heart of suffering itself the means of inspiration and survival.

—**Winston Churchill**

Great events make me quiet and calm, and little trifles fidget me and irritate my nerves.

—**Queen Victoria**

We draw our strength from the very despair in which we have been forced to live. We shall endure.

—**Cesar Chavez**

The English nation is never so great as in adversity.

—**Benjamin Disraeli**

To suffer and to endure is the lot of humanity.

—**Pope Leo XIII**

Comfort and prosperity have never enriched the world as much as adversity has.

—**Billy Graham**

I have learned over the years that when one's mind is made up, this diminishes fear; knowing what must be done does away with fear.

—**Rosa Parks**

I learned that courage was not the absence of fear, but the triumph over it. The brave man is not he who does not feel afraid, but he who conquers that fear.

—**Nelson Mandela**

Although the world is full of suffering, it is also full of the overcoming of it.

—**Helen Keller**

I think the years I have spent in prison have been the most formative and important in my life because of the discipline, the sensations, but chiefly the opportunity to think clearly, to try to understand things.

—Jawaharlal Nehru

Those things that hurt, instruct.

—Benjamin Franklin

Courage is more exhilarating than fear and in the long run it is easier. We do not have to become heroes overnight. Just a step at a time, meeting each thing that comes up, seeing it is not as dreadful as it appeared, discovering we have the strength to stare it down.

—Eleanor Roosevelt

The ultimate measure of a man is not where he stands in moments of comfort and convenience, but where he stands at times of challenge and controversy.

—Martin Luther King, Jr.

Hold your head high, stick your chest out. You can make it. It gets dark sometimes but morning comes. . . . Keep hope alive.

—**Jesse Jackson**

Hope in the face of difficulty, hope in the face of uncertainty, the audacity of hope: In the end, that is God's greatest gift to us, the bedrock of this nation, a belief in things not seen, a belief that there are better days ahead.

—**Barack Obama**

Hope is like peace. It is not a gift from God. It is a gift only we can give one another.

—**Elie Wiesel**

Hope is like a road in the country; there was never a road, but when many people walk on it, the road comes into existence.

—**Lin Yutang**

When I despair, I remember that all through history the way of truth and love has always won. There have been tyrants and murderers and for a time they seem invincible, but in the end, they always fall—think of it, always.

—**Mahatma Gandhi**

It is often when night looks darkest, it is often before the fever breaks that one senses the gathering momentum for change, when one feels that resurrection of hope in the midst of despair and apathy.

—**Hillary Rodham Clinton**

Hope is being able to see that there is light despite all of the darkness.

—**Desmond Tutu**

POVERTY AND WEALTH

The test of our progress is not whether we add more to the abundance of those who have much; it is whether we provide enough for those who have too little.

—**Franklin D. Roosevelt**

Overcoming poverty is not a gesture of charity. It is the protection of a fundamental human right, the right to dignity and a decent life.

—**Nelson Mandela**

The defining and ongoing innovations of this age—biotechnology, the computer, the Internet—give us a chance we've never had before to end extreme poverty and end death from preventable disease.

—**Bill Gates**

In imitation of our Master, we Christians are called to confront the poverty of our brothers and sisters, to touch it, to make it our own and to take practical steps to alleviate it.

—**Pope Francis**

Poverty often deprives a Man of all Spirit and Virtue; 'Tis hard for an empty Bag to stand up-right.

—**Benjamin Franklin**

Poverty must not be a bar to learning, and learning must offer an escape from poverty.

—**Lyndon B. Johnson**

We must talk about poverty, because people insulated by their own comfort lose sight of it.

—**Dorothy Day**

Poor people have a much, much greater capacity for solving their own problems than most people give them credit for.

—**Wilma Mankiller**

The world is a dangerous place, not because of those who do evil, but because of those who look on and do nothing.

—**Albert Einstein**

There is no dignity quite so impressive, and no one independence quite so important, as living within your means.

—**Calvin Coolidge**

There must be a reason why some people can afford to live well. They must have worked for it. I only feel angry when I see waste. When I see people throwing away things we could use.

—Mother Teresa

What material success does is provide you with the ability to concentrate on other things that really matter. And that is being able to make a difference, not only in your own life, but in other people's lives.

—Oprah Winfrey

There is nothing wrong with men possessing riches. The wrong comes when riches possess men.

—Billy Graham

Money has no utility to me beyond a certain point. Its utility is entirely in building an organization and getting the resources out to the poorest in the world.

—Bill Gates

Something is very wrong when, last year, the top twenty-five hedge fund managers earned more than the combined income of four hundred twenty-five thousand public school teachers. We have to get our priorities right.

—Bernie Sanders

I need to pay higher taxes. I've paid, in absolute, more taxes, over ten billion (dollars), than anyone else, but, you know, the government should require the people in my position to pay significantly higher taxes.

—**Bill Gates**

A land where millionaires and billionaires have never had it so good, while tens of millions struggle just to survive is not what Christianity is about. It's not what Judaism is about. And it's not what America is supposed to be about.

—**Bernie Sanders**

In this world it is possible to achieve great material wealth, to live an opulent life. But a life built upon those things alone leaves a shallow legacy.

—**Cesar Chavez**

THE WORLD AROUND US

We are citizens of the world; and the tragedy of our times is that we do not know this.

—**Woodrow Wilson**

To realize the full possibilities of this economy, we must reach beyond our own borders to shape the revolution that is tearing down barriers and building new networks among nations and individuals and economies and cultures: globalization. It's the central reality of our time.

—**Bill Clinton**

The world has changed far more in the past 100 years than in any other century in history. The reason is not political or economic but technological—technologies that flowed directly from advances in basic science.

—**Stephen Hawking**

Life is as dear to a mute creature as it is to man. Just as one wants happiness and fears pain, just as one wants to live and not die, so do other creatures.

—**Dalai Lama**

We are not on earth to guard a museum, but to tend a blooming garden full of life.

—**Pope John XXIII**

Let no one be discouraged by the belief that there is nothing one person can do against the enormous array of the world's ills, misery, ignorance, and violence. Few will have the greatness to bend history, but each of us can work to change a small portion of events. And in the total of all those acts will be written the history of a generation.

—**Robert F. Kennedy**

The old Lakota was wise. He knew that a man's heart, away from nature, becomes hard; he knew that lack of respect for growing, living things soon led to lack of respect for humans too. So he kept his children close to nature's softening influence.

—**Luther Standing Bear**

Please, I would like to ask all those who have positions of responsibility in economic, political and social life, and all men and women of good will: Let us be "protectors" of creation, protectors of God's plan inscribed in nature, protectors of one another and of the environment. Let us not allow omens of destruction and death to accompany the advance of this world.

—**Pope Francis**

We won't have a society if we destroy the environment.

—**Margaret Mead**

Today, more than ever before, life must be characterized by a sense of universal responsibility, not only nation to nation and human to human, but also human to other forms of life.

—**Dalai Lama**

Protecting the earth is not an intellectual exercise, it's a sacred duty.

—**Wilma Mankiller**

Climate change knows no borders. It will not stop before the Pacific islands and the whole of the international community here has to shoulder a responsibility to bring about a sustainable development.

—**Angela Merkel**

It has become appallingly obvious that our technology has exceeded our humanity.

—**Albert Einstein**

We must learn to live together as brothers or perish together as fools.

—**Martin Luther King, Jr.**

Optimism is a huge asset. We can always use more of it. But optimism isn't a belief that things will automatically get better; it's a conviction that we can make things better.

—**Melinda Gates**

As long as poverty, injustice and gross inequality exist in our world, none of us can truly rest.

—**Nelson Mandela**

Today's real borders are not between nations, but between powerful and powerless, free and fettered, privileged and humiliated. Today, no walls can separate humanitarian or human rights crises in one part of the world from national security crises in another.

—**Kofi Annan**

Saving our planet, lifting people out of poverty, advancing economic growth . . . these are one and the same fight.

—**Ban Ki-moon**

Be ashamed to die until you have won some victory for humanity.

—**Horace Mann**

To put the world right in order, we must first put the nation in order; to put the nation in order, we must first put the family in order; to put the family in order, we must first cultivate our personal life; we must first set our hearts right.

—**Confucius**

THE WISDOM OF LEADERS

Genius is sometimes only an instinct which is incapable of being perfected. In most cases the art of judging correctly is perfected only through observation and experience. A good thought is not always associated with good judgment, but good judgment always presupposes a good thought.

—**Napoleon Bonaparte**

You must not consult the opinions and judgments of merely the present generation, but also those of future people. And yet posterity's judgment, freed from detraction and malice, will be the more genuine.

—**Cicero**

I am no lover of pompous title, but only desire that my name be recorded in a line or two, which shall briefly express my name, my virginity, the years of my reign, the reformation of religion under it, and my preservation of peace.

—**Queen Elizabeth I**

Mankind will endure when the world appreciates the logic of diversity.

—**Indira Gandhi**

You have to trust in something—your gut, destiny, life, karma, whatever. This approach has never let me down, and it has made all the difference in my life.

—**Steve Jobs**

Fight for the things that you care about, but do it in a way that will lead others to join you.

—**Ruth Bader Ginsburg**

It is my firm belief that the solution to all problems lies in dialogue. Earlier, it was believed that force indicates power. Now, power must come through the strength of ideas and the effective dialogue.

—**Narendra Modi**

It is impossible for peace to exist without dialogue. All the wars, all the strife, all the unsolved problems over which we clash are due to a lack of dialogue. When there is a problem, talk: this makes peace.

—**Pope Francis**

My whole life, whether it be long or short, shall be devoted to your service and the service of our great imperial family to which we all belong. But I shall not have the strength to carry out this resolution alone unless you join in it with me.

—**Queen Elizabeth II**

After leaving the Kremlin . . . my conscience was clear. The promise I gave to the people when I started the process of perestroika was kept: I gave them freedom.

—**Mikhail Gorbachev**

For, what is a family without a steward, a ship without a pilot, a flock without a shepherd, a body without a head, the same, I think, is a kingdom without the health and safety of a good monarch.

—**Queen Elizabeth I**

When we hate our enemies, we are giving them power over us: power over our sleep, our appetites, our blood pressure, our health, and our happiness.

—**Dale Carnegie**

We live in a land made of ideals, not blood and soil. We are the custodians of those ideals at home, and their champion abroad. We have done great good in the world. That leadership has had its costs, but we have become incomparably powerful and wealthy as we did. We have a moral obligation to continue in our just cause, and we would bring more than shame on ourselves if we don't. We will not thrive in a world where our leadership and ideals are absent. We wouldn't deserve to.

—**John McCain**

Don't give in to complacency and cynicism. Don't ignore what is bad, but concentrate on building what is good.

—**John Glenn**

In my humble opinion, non-cooperation with evil is as much a duty as is cooperation with good.

—**Mahatma Gandhi**

But humanity's greatest advances are not in its discoveries—but in how those discoveries are applied to reduce inequity. Whether through democracy, strong public education, quality health care, or broad economic opportunity—reducing inequity is the highest human achievement.

—**Bill Gates**

We must restore hope to young people, help the old, be open to the future, spread love. Be poor among the poor. We need to include the excluded and preach peace.

—**Pope Francis**

I could not, at any age, be content to take my place by the fireside and simply look on. Life was meant to be lived. Curiosity must be kept alive. One must never, for whatever reason, turn his back on life.

—**Eleanor Roosevelt**

When you arise in the morning, think of what a privilege it is to be alive—to breathe, to think, to enjoy, to love.

—Marcus Aurelius

No one is born hating another person because of the color of his skin, or his background, or his religion. People must learn to hate, and if they can learn to hate, they can be taught to love, for love comes more naturally to the human heart than its opposite.

—Nelson Mandela

CONTRIBUTORS

Hank Aaron *(b. 1934)* — American professional baseball player, civil rights activist, and baseball executive

John Adams *(1735–1826)* — 2nd President of the United States, 1st Vice President of the United States, lawyer, diplomat, and statesman

John Quincy Adams *(1767–1848)* — 6th President of the United States, diplomat, ambassador, statesman; son of John Adams

Chimamanda Ngozi Adichie *(b. 1977)* — Nigerian writer and activist

Madeleine Albright *(b. 1937)* — Czech-born American politician, diplomat, and U.S. Secretary of State

Alexander the Great *(356–323 BCE)* — Macedonian ruler

Muhammad Ali *(1942–2016)* — American boxer, activist, and philanthropist

Marian Anderson *(1897–1993)* — American opera singer and civil rights activist

Kofi Annan *(b. 1938)* — Ghanaian diplomat and 7th Secretary-General of the United Nations

Susan B. Anthony *(1820–1906)* — American activist and key figure in the U.S. women's rights movement

St. Thomas Aquinas *(c. 1225–1274)* — Italian Dominican friar, priest, philosopher, theologian, and Doctor of the Church

Arthur Ashe *(1943–1993)* — American tennis player and humanitarian

St. Augustine *(354–430 CE)* — African-born theologian, priest, bishop, and Doctor of the Church

Marcus Aurelius *(121–180 CE)* — Roman emperor

Ella J. Baker *(1903–1986)* — American civil rights activist

Clara Barton *(1821–1912)* — American nurse, teacher, and founder of the American Red Cross

Warren Bennis *(1925–2014)* — American scholar, organizational consultant, and writer

Mary McLeod Bethune *(1875–1955)* — American educator, civil rights and women's rights activist, government official, presidential advisor, and businesswoman

Jeff Bezos *(b. 1964)* —American entrepreneur, investor, and philanthropist

Benazir Bhutto *(1953–2007)* — Pakistani politician, activist, and Prime Minister of Pakistan

Joe Biden *(b. 1942)* —American politician and 47th Vice President of the United States

Stephen Biko *(1946–1977)* — South African anti-apartheid activist

Elizabeth Blackwell *(1821–1910)* — American physician

Tony Blair *(b. 1953)* — British politician and prime minister

Michael Bloomberg *(b. 1942)* — American business magnate, politician, and philanthropist

Simón Bolívar *(1783–1830)* — Venezuelan military and political leader

Napoleon Bonaparte *(1769–1821)* — French statesman and military leader

Cory Booker *(b. 1969)* — American politician and activist

Bill Bradley *(b. 1943)* — American politician and former professional basketball player

Omar Bradley *(1893–1981)* — American general, first Chairman of the Joint Chiefs of Staff

Louis D. Brandeis *(1856–1941)* — American lawyer and U.S. Supreme Court Justice

James Buchanan *(1791–1868)* —15th President of the United States

Edmund Burke *(1729–1797)* — Irish philosopher and statesman

Tarana Burke *(b. 1973)* — American civil rights and women's rights activist

James MacGregor Burns *(1918–2014)* — American historian, political scientist, and writer

George W. Bush *(b. 1946)* — 43rd President of the United States and painter

Julius Caesar *(100–44 BCE)* — Roman general and statesman

Geoffrey Canada *(b. 1952)* — American educator, writer, and social activist

Thomas Carlyle *(1795–1881)* — Scottish historian and political philosopher

Andrew Carnegie *(1835–1919)* — Scottish-American business magnate, industrialist, and philanthropist

Dale Carnegie *(1888–1955)* — American writer, lecturer, and self-help pioneer

Jimmy Carter *(b. 1924)* — 39th President of the United States, humanitarian, and diplomat

Carrie Chapman Catt *(1859–1947)* — American women's suffrage leader

Cesar Chavez *(1927–1993)* — American labor leader, civil rights activist, and co-founder of the National Farm Workers Association

Winston Churchill *(1874–1965)* — British statesman and prime minister

Bill Clinton *(b. 1946)* — 42nd President of the United States, humanitarian, and philanthropist

Hillary Rodham Clinton *(b. 1947)* — American politician, U.S. Secretary of State, U.S. Senator, First Lady of the United States, and first female presidential candidate of a major political party

Susan Collins *(b. 1952)* — American politician

James Comey *(b. 1960)* — American lawyer and 7th Director of the F.B.I.

Confucius *(551–479 BCE)* — Chinese philosopher

Charles Cooley *(1864–1929)* — American sociologist and academic

Calvin Coolidge *(1872–1933)* — 30th President of the United States

Marie Curie *(1867–1934)* — French-Polish physicist and chemist

Dalai Lama (Tenzin Gyatso) *(b. 1935)* — Tibetan monk and religious leader

Dorothy Day *(1897–1980)* — American journalist and social activist in the Catholic Worker Movement

Charles de Gaulle *(1890–1970)* — French general and politician

John Dewey *(1859–1952)* — American philosopher, psychologist, and educator

Mahatma Gandhi *(1869–1948)* — Indian nationalist leader and activist

James A. Garfield *(1831–1881)* — 20th President of the United States

Alicia Garza *(b. 1981)* — American activist and writer, co-founder of the Black Lives Matter movement

Bill Gates *(b. 1955)* — American business magnate, humanitarian, and philanthropist

Melinda Gates *(b. 1964)* — American businesswoman, humanitarian, and philanthropist

Kirsten Gillibrand *(b. 1966)* — American politician and attorney

Ruth Bader Ginsburg *(b. 1933)* — American lawyer, academic, and U.S. Supreme Court Justice

John Glenn *(1921–2016)* — American aviator, engineer, astronaut, and politician

Johann Wolfgang von Goethe *(1749–1832)* — German poet and dramatist

Mikhail Gorbachev *(b. 1931)* — Russian politician and social activist

Billy Graham *(1918–2018)* — American evangelist and Christian minister

Katharine Graham *(1917–2001)* — American newspaper publisher

Ulysses S. Grant *(1822–1885)* — 18th President of the United States, General in Chief of Union Armies during the Civil War

Nikki Haley *(b. 1972)* — American politician and U.S. Ambassador to the United Nations

Alexander Hamilton *(1755–1804)* — American statesman

Kamala Harris *(b. 1964)* — American politician and lawyer

Stephen Hawking *(1942–2018)* — English theoretical physicist, cosmologist, and writer

Abraham Joshua Heschel *(1907–1972)* — Polish-born American rabbi and theologian

Anita Hill *(b. 1956)* — American attorney, academic, and writer

Oveta Culp Hobby *(1905–1995)* — American editor, publisher, first secretary of the Department of Health, Education and Welfare, and first commanding officer of the Women's Army Corps

Grace Hopper *(1906–1992)* — American computer scientist and U.S. Navy rear admiral

Jesse Jackson *(b. 1941)* — American civil rights activist, political activist, minister, and politician

John Jay *(1745–1829)* — American statesman, diplomat, politician, and first Chief Justice of the U.S. Supreme Court

Thomas Jefferson *(1743–1826)* — 3rd President of the United States and principal author of the Declaration of Independence

Steve Jobs *(1955–2011)* — American entrepreneur, business magnate, and inventor

Pope John XXIII *(1881–1963)* — 261st pope of the Catholic Church and Catholic saint

Pope John Paul II *(1920–2005)* — 264th pope of the Catholic Church and Catholic saint

Lyndon B. Johnson *(1908–1973)* — 36th President of the United States

Mother Jones (Mary Harris Jones) *(1830–1930)* — Irish-American labor organizer and humanitarian

Carl Jung *(1875–1961)* — Swiss psychiatrist, psychoanalyst, and founder of analytical psychology

Colin Kaepernick *(b. 1987)* — American professional football player and activist

Helen Keller *(1880–1968)* — American writer, activist, educator, and lecturer

John F. Kennedy *(1917–1963)* — 35th President of the United States

Robert F. Kennedy *(1925–1968)* — American politician and lawyer who served as U.S. Attorney General during JFK administration, civil rights activist, assassinated during his presidential run

Ted Kennedy *(1932–2009)* — American politician and social activist

Ban Ki-moon *(b. 1944)* — South Korean diplomat and 8th Secretary-General of the United Nations

Billie Jean King *(b. 1943)* — American professional tennis player and social justice and human rights activist

Coretta Scott King *(1927–2006)* — American activist and wife of Dr. Martin Luther King, Jr.

Martin Luther King, Jr. *(1929–1968)* — American clergyman and prominent leader of mass civil rights movement from 1950s until his assassination in 1968

Marquis de Lafayette (Gilbert du Motier) *(1757–1834)* — French aristocrat and military officer who fought in the Revolutionary War

Emma Lazarus *(1849–1887)* — American poet and writer

Pope Leo XIII *(1810–1903)* — 256th pope of the Catholic Church

John Lewis *(b. 1940)* — American politician, civil rights leader, and human rights activist

Abraham Lincoln *(1809–1865)* — 16th President of the United States, statesman, and lawyer

John Locke *(1632–1704)* — English philosopher

Douglas MacArthur *(1880–1964)* — American general

James Madison *(1751–1836)* — 4th President of the United States and statesman

Malcolm X *(1925–1965)* — American religious leader and human rights activist

Nelson Mandela *(1918–2013)* — South African political leader, activist, humanitarian, philanthropist, and lawyer

Wilma Mankiller *(1945–2010)* — Native American activist and first woman chief of the Cherokee Nation

Horace Mann *(1796–1859)* — American educational reformer and politician

George C. Marshall *(1880–1959)* — American statesman, Chief of Staff of the U.S. Army, U.S. Secretary of State, and U.S. Secretary of Defense

Thurgood Marshall *(1908–1993)* — American civil rights activist, lawyer, and U.S. Supreme Court Justice

John C. Maxwell *(b. 1947)* — American writer, speaker, and pastor

John McCain *(b. 1936)* — American politician, naval aviator, and prisoner of war during Vietnam War

Margaret Mead *(1901–1978)* — American cultural anthropologist and writer

Golda Meir *(1898–1978)* — Founder of the State of Israel and 4th Prime Minister of Israel

Angela Merkel *(b. 1954)* — German politician and Chancellor of Germany

Thomas Merton *(1915–1968)* — American Catholic writer, mystic, and theologian

Narendra Modi *(b. 1950)* — Indian politician and current Prime Minister of India

Bernard Montgomery *(1887–1976)* — British general

Lucretia Mott *(1793–1880)* — American abolitionist and women's rights activist

Elon Musk *(b. 1971)* — South African–born business magnate, engineer, inventor, and investor

Ralph Nader *(b. 1934)* — American political activist, consumer advocate, environmentalist, and attorney

Jawaharlal Nehru *(1889–1964)* — Indian politician and first Prime Minister of India

Horatio Nelson *(1758–1805)* — British flag officer in the Royal Navy

Indra Nooyi *(b. 1955)* — Indian-American business executive

Barack Obama *(b. 1961)* — 44th President of the United States, lawyer, academic, writer, and humanitarian

Michelle Obama *(b. 1964)* — American lawyer, writer, humanitarian, and First Lady of the United States

Sandra Day O'Connor *(b.1930)* — American U.S. Supreme Court Justice

Jacqueline Kennedy Onassis *(1929–1994)* — American activist, editor, writer, and First Lady of the United States

Thomas P. "Tip" O'Neill *(1912 –1994)* — American politician

J. Robert Oppenheimer *(1904–1967)* — American theoretical physicist

Thomas Paine *(1737–1809)* — English-born political philosopher and writer

Emmeline Pankhurst *(1858–1928)* — English activist

Rosa Parks *(1913–2005)* — American civil rights activist

George S. Patton *(1885–1945)* — American general

Alice Paul *(1885–1977)* — American women's suffrage leader

Norman Vincent Peale *(1898–1993)* — American minister and best-selling author

Nancy Pelosi *(b. 1940)* — American politician

John J. Pershing *(1860–1948)* — American general

Colin Powell *(b. 1937)* — American retired general, U.S. National Security Advisor, Chairman of the Joint Chiefs of Staff, U.S. Secretary of State, and statesman

Ronald Reagan *(1911–2004)* — 40th President of the United States

Condoleezza Rice *(b. 1954)* — American academic, diplomat, writer, and U.S. Secretary of State

Jackie Robinson *(1919–1972)* — American professional baseball player and first African American to play in Major League Baseball

Eleanor Roosevelt *(1884–1962)* — American humanitarian, political activist, and longest-serving First Lady of the United States

Franklin D. Roosevelt *(1882–1945)* — 32nd President of the United States and the only president elected four times

Theodore Roosevelt *(1858–1919)* — 26th President of the United States, writer, naturalist, soldier, and statesman

Sheryl Sandberg *(b. 1969)* — American business executive, activist, and writer

Bernie Sanders *(b. 1941)* — American politician and activist

H. Norman Schwarzkopf, Jr. *(1934–2012)* — American general

Margaret Chase Smith *(1897–1995)* — American politician

Socrates *(c. 470–399 BCE)* — Greek philosopher

Aleksandr Solzhenitsyn *(1918–2008)* — Russian novelist, historian, and political activist

Herbert Spencer *(1820–1903)* — English philosopher and sociologist

Benjamin Spock *(1903–1998)* — American pediatrician, writer, and political activist

Luther Standing Bear *(1868–1939)* — Native American chief of Oglala Lakota tribe, educator, philosopher, writer, and actor

Elizabeth Cady Stanton *(1815–1902)* — American social activist, abolitionist, and pioneer of the U.S. women's rights movement

Gloria Steinem *(b. 1934)* — American writer, journalist, and political and social activist

Adlai Stevenson *(1900–1965)* — American lawyer, politician, and diplomat

Martha Stewart *(b. 1941)* — American businesswoman, writer, and television host

Harriet Beecher Stowe *(1811–1896)* — American writer and abolitionist

St. Teresa of Ávila *(1515–1582)* — Spanish mystic, Roman Catholic nun, founder, spiritual writer, Roman Catholic saint, and Doctor of the Church

St. Teresa of Calcutta (Mother Teresa) *(1910–1997)* — Albanian-born Roman Catholic nun, founder, and Roman Catholic saint

Margaret Thatcher *(1925–2013)* — British politician and Prime Minister of the United Kingdom

Harry S. Truman *(1884–1972)* — 33rd President of the United States and statesman

Sojourner Truth *(1797–1883)* — American abolitionist and women's rights activist

Harriet Tubman *(1820–1913)* — American abolitionist and humanitarian

Desmond Tutu *(b. 1931)* — South African human rights activist and retired Anglican bishop

Lao Tzu *(c. 604–531 bce)* — Chinese philosopher and poet

Gloria Vanderbilt *(b. 1924)* — American artist, writer, heiress, and entrepreneur

Queen Victoria *(1819–1901)* — British monarch

Otto von Bismarck *(1815–1898)* — Prussian statesman

Earl Warren *(1891–1974)* — American lawyer, politician, and Chief Justice of the U.S. Supreme Court

Elizabeth Warren *(b. 1949)* — American academic, politician, and writer

Booker T. Washington *(1856–1915)* — American educator, writer, activist, and most prominent African-American leader of his time

George Washington *(1732–1799)* — 1st President of the United States, statesman, and Commander-in-Chief of the Continental Army

Martha Washington *(1731–1802)* — First Lady of the United States

Elie Wiesel *(1928–2016)* — Romanian-born American writer, professor, political activist, and humanitarian

Woodrow Wilson *(1856–1924)* — 28th President of the United States, statesman, and academic

Oprah Winfrey *(b. 1954)* — American media mogul, talk-show host, actress, producer, and philanthropist

Sarah Winnemucca *(c. 1844–1891)* — Native American writer, activist, and educator

Janet Yellen *(b. 1946)* — American economist

Malala Yousafzai *(b. 1997)* — Pakistani activist and writer

Lin Yutang *(1895–1976)* — Chinese writer and inventor